Essentials of
Performance Management
and
Performance Appraisal

Books by Shyam Bhatawdekar and Dr Kalpana Bhatawdekar

Management, Business, Self-help and Personality Development Books

1. HSoftware (Human Software) (The Only Key to Higher Effectiveness) https://www.amazon.com/dp/B005G32JRI
2. Sensitive Stories of Corporate World (Management Case Studies) https://www.amazon.com/dp/B004KABBMM
3. Sensitive Stories of Corporate World (Volume 2) (Management Case Studies) https://www.amazon.com/dp/B072PT1JGP
4. Sensitive Stories of Corporate World (Volumes 1 & 2 Combined) (Management Case Studies) https://www.amazon.com/dp/B07G5G4WRP
5. Classic Management Games, Exercises, Energizers and Icebreakers https://www.amazon.com/dp/B004OEKF0I
6. Classic Management Games, Exercises, Energizers and Icebreakers (Volume 2) https://www.amazon.com/dp/B007CIESMY
7. Classic Team Building Games, Exercises, Energizers and Icebreakers https://www.amazon.com/dp/B00MJC8SPQ
8. 101 Classic Management Games, Exercises, Energizers and Icebreakers https://www.amazon.com/dp/B07HFZ19V4
9. Stress? No Way!! (Handbook on Stress Management) https://www.amazon.com/dp/B005LV37J0
10. HSoftware (Shyam Bhatawdekar's Effectiveness Model) https://www.amazon.com/dp/B005IOS2TQ
11. Competency Management (Competency Matrix and Competencies) https://www.amazon.com/dp/B00VNTZKK2

12. Soft Skills You Can't Do Without (Goal Setting, Time Management, Assertiveness and Anger Management) https://www.amazon.com/dp/B00KE5WUXQ
13. Essentials of Work Study (Method Study and Work Measurement) https://www.amazon.com/dp/B008RYYWJQ
14. Essentials of Time Management (Taking Control of Your Life) https://www.amazon.com/dp/B009WXI1ZW
15. Essentials of 5S Housekeeping
https://www.amazon.com/dp/B00A6HCVRM
16. Essentials of Quality Circles
https://www.amazon.com/dp/B00ACHOHGE
17. Essentials of Goal Setting
https://www.amazon.com/dp/B00AP1DEXO
18. Essentials of Anger Management
https://www.amazon.com/dp/B00AZFLIII
19. Essentials of Assertive Behavior
https://www.amazon.com/dp/B00C5UMCEU
20. Essentials of Performance Management and Performance Appraisal https://www.amazon.com/dp/B00DA06UTM
21. Health Essentials (Health Is Wealth)
https://www.amazon.com/dp/B00E5IFCSS
22. Essentials of Effective Communication
https://www.amazon.com/dp/B071XJ823H
23. The Romance of Intimacy (How to Enhance Intimacy in a Relationship?)
https://www.amazon.com/dp/B007NGBBOI

Novels, Stories, Biographies and Travelogues

24. The Peace Crusaders (Novel: how the peace crusaders established permanent peace on a war strewn planet?) https://www.amazon.com/dp/B00Q3OBIY4
25. Love Knows No Bounds (Novel: a refreshingly different love story. Also available with the title "Good People") https://www.amazon.com/dp/B00HO2KFMA
26. The New World Order (Emergence of a Star) (Novel: thriller, mystery, adventure, drama)
https://www.amazon.com/dp/B085MYGH63

27. Funny (and Not So Funny) Short Stories
https://www.amazon.com/dp/B004MDLTPQ

28. Stories Children Will Love (Volume 1: Bhanu-Shanu-Kaju-Biju and Dholu Ram Gadbad Singh)
https://www.amazon.com/dp/B0071J74CA

29. My Father (Biography)
https://www.amazon.com/dp/B019A4L8KM

30. Travelogue: Scandinavia, Russia
https://www.amazon.com/dp/B008QYMS3E

31. Travelogue: Europe https://www.amazon.com/dp/B01JD2255Y

32. Travelogue: Central Europe
https://www.amazon.com/dp/B07YVFND27

33. सीमाओं के परे: एक अलग प्रेम कहानी (Hindi edition of "Love Knows Bounds") https://www.amazon.com/dp/B07D6BQXYW

34. अमन के सिपाही (Hindi edition of "The Peace Crusaders") https://www.amazon.com/dp/B07RC4CV2R

35. अभिजात प्रेम: एक वेगळी प्रेम कथा (Marathi edition of "Love Knows Bounds") https://www.amazon.com/dp/B089FKP6GC

To Our Family

Shyam Bhatawdekar   Dr Kalpana Bhatawdekar

Performance management and performance appraisal are often confused with each other. Additionally, these are often thought as management gimmicks best relegated to HR guys of an organization.

The truth is that in today's highly competitive environment performance management and therefore, performance appraisal have become strategic interventions. Managers and employees at every level and from every department of every organization will become more effective individually and organizationally if they start using these two interventions seriously as their important management tools.

This book therefore should become an important reference document for every manager and every employee. To assimilate the required knowledge on the subject quickly only the essential and value-adding aspects of performance management and performance appraisal have been included in the book leaving out the nonessential, unnecessary and non-value adding stuff.

The authors of the book are top-notch business executives, successful entrepreneurs, highly sought-after business and management consultants, eminent management gurus and scholars, authentic human behavior experts and prolific authors. And so, the book becomes an authentic document on the subject.

To read more by the authors, refer their website: http://management-universe.blogspot.com

Essentials of

Performance Management
and
Performance Appraisal

Shyam Bhatawdekar
Dr Kalpana Bhatawdekar

Published by Publishing Division of

Prodcons Group

8, Pranjal Society, Shiv Tirth Nagar, Paud Road, Pune 411038 (India)

Email: prodcons@prodcons.com

For other web publications, refer: http://management-universe.blogspot.com

Contents

1. Performance Management: The Felt Need- 10
2. Performance Management: Unified Approach- 11
3. Why Performance Management?- 12
4. Benefits of Performance Management System- 14
5. Generic Performance Management Model- 15
6. Performance Appraisal: Introduction- 18
7. Why Performance Appraisal?- 19
8. Uses of Performance Appraisal/Evaluation in Other HRM and Organizational Functions- 20
9. Evolution of Performance Appraisal and Performance Management- 21
10. Many Appraisal Systems- 31
11. Pitfalls in Performance Appraisal in Practice- 33
12. Superior Most Systems- 39
13. Requirements of a Good Appraisal System- 40
14. Rating Scales- 41
15. Post Appraisal Actions- 42
16. Designing a Performance Appraisal Form- 45
17. Performance Review Meeting- 51
18. Frequency of Appraisals- 54
19. Performance Appraisal: Dynamic Process- 55
20. Anti Views on Performance Appraisal- 55

Essentials of Performance Management and Performance Appraisal

Performance Management: The Felt Need

Use of performance management dates back to 1940. Originally it was developed and used to justify whether the remuneration paid to an employee was commensurate with his performance. Over the years many sophistications were brought into this system.

In more serious ways performance management took off as a result of ever-increasing competitiveness in the local and global market spheres. Due to these competitive pressures organizations felt the need for a comprehensive performance management system that could improve overall productivity and performance effectiveness on an ongoing basis and thus a unified approach was conceived.

Organizations use many types of resources like land, machines, materials, money, information, time as well as human beings. Performance management that emphasizes

11

performance management of human resources distinguishes itself as a more successful organization.

The performance management system integrates all the departments of an organization and steers them toward an organization's ever increasing/changing goals year after year. The system uses processes resulting in a work environment where the employees of an organization are enabled and motivated to perform their best.

Armstrong and Baron (1998) defined it as a "strategic and integrated approach to increase the effectiveness of companies by improving the performance of the people who work in them and by developing the capabilities of teams and individual contributors."

Performance Management: Unified Approach

Performance management is a:

- Wholesome unified approach towards looking after the business and the people together.
- Unified HRM approach that integrates a formal review of employee performance within the

framework of desired performance of an organization. It acts as a linking pin starting with the mission and ultimate goals of the organization, aligning business units, teams and individuals, understanding what is expected from them and all of this leading to aligning the individuals towards achievement of organizational goals.

- Integrated process for improving employee performance directed towards ensuring that the organizational goals (that get enhanced every year) are met and ultimately achieving them.

- Integration of systems and processes of setting goals, determining performance standards, assigning the work, evaluating/appraising the work performed by the employees, training/developing them by determining the training/development needs and rewarding them appropriately.

Why Performance Management?

The major reasons to turn to performance management are:

- Enhanced employee performance in the organizational context requires more organizational support in terms of goal setting systems, learning/training systems, appraisal systems and rewards systems in addition to mere self motivation of the employees. A well-designed and well-implemented performance management system fulfills these requirements.

- In globally competitive environment there is a need for continuous improvement of the performance of an organization, which in turn depends on the continuous improvement of the performance of its employees year after year. Performance management aims at that. It transforms human resource management into a result and process driven strategic business function by aligning employee goals and actions with the organizational strategy.

- Performance management system makes performance appraisal more objective and useful. Otherwise, many a time, the traditional performance appraisal carried out in isolation may prove to be counterproductive. Performance management system is capable of understanding the true strengths and weaknesses at every organizational level.

- Performance management focuses the efforts of the entire organization and particularly the efforts of its human resources to the ultimate goals of the organization. Thus, it facilitates retention of top performers and development of low performers.

Benefits of Performance Management System

Following benefits may be accrued by an organization by effectively implementing the performance management system:

- Aligns employee goals with organizational goals thus facilitating achievement of improved results in terms of increased customers, higher sales, improved profits and overall growth.
- Reduced overall costs and wastages.
- Contains project overruns.
- Effective, speedy and open communication throughout the organization with lots of transparency.
- Higher trust of employees in organization's performance evaluation and rewards systems.
- Improved motivation and morale of the people.

- Better training and development resulting in higher levels of competencies and skill sets.
- Better overall management review and control.

Generic Performance Management Model

For achieving a complete integration, a generic performance management model is given below. However, every organization can customize it to its specific objectives and requirements.

The process steps are given in a logical sequence:

Step 1. Planning: Planning includes planning and deciding about:

1. Vision and mission
2. Objectives
3. Core competencies (of the organization)
4. Critical success factors
5. Key performance indicators
6. Strategies
7. Organizational structure
8. Skills and competencies (required of individuals

working for the organization)

9. Position and job descriptions
10. Objectives/goals of each individual working for the organization
11. Plans of action
12. Induction, mentoring, training and developing the employees

Step 2. Measuring and Rating: This step relates to measuring actual performance of an organization, it's departments and people against the planned performance. Evaluating and rating of the employees are important aspects. So, it involves:

13. Achievement measurement as against planned
14. Performance review or performance appraisal of employees and rating them
15. Assessments of skill and competency gaps and gap analysis

Step 3. Developing: It emphasizes training and development of people based on the outcomes of earlier step of measuring and rating. It includes:

16. Individual development plans based on the organizational gaps in critical success factors of the organization (e.g. the gaps could be in quality or cost competitiveness or customer relations or enhancing team effort/communication etc)

17. Training and other developmental initiatives like job rotation, job enrichment, transfers, task force assignments, foreign assignments etc based on competency evaluation of the employees and organizational requirements

18. Individual counseling, coaching and mentoring

Step 4: Awards and Rewards: It is necessary to keep up the motivation and morale levels of the people at the highest levels. Therefore, the performance management must include wholesome schemes of:

19. Recognition and rewards
20. Career plans and succession plans

Of the above-mentioned steps of performance management model, in the subsequent paragraphs we are now going to get into the details of the step called the "performance appraisal" which is very crucial in measuring the actual performance of individual employees against their planned performance (which is finally reflected in organizational performance). It is a well-known fact that what can be measured only can be further improved and ongoing improvements are essential for progress of an organization.

Performance Appraisal: Introduction

Performance appraisal is also termed as employee appraisal, performance evaluation and performance review.

Performance appraisal is an important and indispensable subset or part of the overall performance management system. Performance appraisal is necessary to measure the performance of the employees and the organization to check the progress towards the desired goals and aims.

People differ in their abilities and their aptitudes. Therefore, quality and quantity of the same work delivered by different people on the same job can be different. Performance appraisal assesses each employee's abilities, competencies as well as his relative merit and worth to the organization. Performance appraisal rates the employees in terms of their performance, competencies/skills and potentials. Essentially it involves:

- Appraising the employees on how well they did in a given past period, say for past six months or over past one year.
- Appraising the employees for their potentials.
- Performance improvement discussions.
- Career development discussions.

Thus, performance appraisal takes into account the past performance of the employees and focuses on the improvement of the future performance and growth of the employees and therefore that of the organization.

Why Performance Appraisal?

Performance appraisal is used in the modern organizations with the following objectives:

- Finding out the levels of performance of the employees and deciding and awarding appropriate motivational packages to the employees in terms of recognition, salary raise, promotion, special rewards, bonus, profit sharing, stock options etc. Linking compensation to performance is quite a just system.

- Finding out the competency gaps of the employees as compared to what competencies they should have. This helps in training and development needs identification and designing the relevant programs.

- Identifying the areas of organizational weaknesses and strengths and working out appropriate interventions for the training and development of the employees.

- Thus, helping in improvement of employees' effectiveness and efficiency.

- Working out additional development interventions for employees like job rotation, job enrichment, transfers between various sites/offices, foreign assignments etc.

- Chalking out the career progression of the employees based on the analysis of their past performance and future potentials.

Uses of Performance Appraisal/Evaluation in Other HRM and Organizational Functions

- Human resource planning. Also refer: http://human-resource-planning.blogspot.com/ (Human Resource Planning) and http://human-capital-architecture.blogspot.com/ (Human Capital Architecture).

- Recruitment and selection. Also refer: http://recruitment-selection.blogspot.com/ (Recruitment and Selection).
- Training and development. Also refer: http://competency-matrix.blogspot.com/ (Competency Matrix), http://training-function.blogspot.com/ (Training and Development), http://coaching-skill.blogspot.com/ (Coaching), http://mentor-mentorship.blogspot.com/ (Mentoring) and http://counseling-skill.blogspot.com/ (Counseling at Workplace).
- Rewards and compensation. Also refer: http://motivation-people.blogspot.com/ (Motivation).
- Employee and organizational effectiveness improvements.

Evolution of Performance Appraisal and Performance Management

Evolution of performance appraisal and performance

management can be traced through the following stages it underwent:

1. **Stage 1: Confidentiality and subjectivity:** The first phase of employee appraisal was characterized by its confidentiality and subjectivity. The appraisal reports were called "confidential reports" or "annual confidential reports (ACRs)". These were typically filled once in an year by an officer for his direct reports. The officer would rate his employees on various traits thought important for the organization. These traits often times were: job knowledge, experience, productivity, quality of work, reliability/dependability, leadership, sincerity, initiative, dynamism, attendance, punctuality, loyalty, commitment to safety etc. The appraiser would use his judgment and rate the appraisee on scale of 1 to 5 or 1 to 10. Obviously, the subjectivity would creep in. Also feedback of the evaluation thus made was never communicated to the employee.

   Following approaches of performance appraisal of the employees got evolved as the early methods to rate the employees:

- *Easy Appraisal Method or Free Form method:* It involved describing the performance of an employee by his superior in a narrative way. It often included examples and evidences to support the narrative.
- *Straight Ranking Method:* In this approach, the appraiser compared the employees by ranking them from the best to the poorest on the basis of their overall performance.
- *Paired Comparison Method:* Another technique of comparison than the straight ranking method compared each employee with all others in the group, one at a time. After making all the comparisons in this fashion the employees were given the final rankings.
- *Critical Incidents Method:* In this method the evaluator rated the employee on the basis of employee's behavior during the critical events/incidents. For bringing in some objectivity the manager had to note down the critical incidents and the employee behavior as and when they occurred.

- *Field Review:* In this method, a senior member of HR department discussed and interviewed the assessing managers (evaluators) to evaluate and rate their respective direct reports. This approach though quite time-consuming helped to reduce the superiors' personal bias.

- *Checklist Method:* The manager was given a checklist of the descriptions/statements of the expected behavior of the employees on job. The manager rated the employee against these criteria.

- *Graphic Rating Scale:* Here employee's quality and quantity of work were assessed in a graphic scale indicating different degrees of a particular trait. The degrees could be: unsatisfactory, average, above average, outstanding etc. The factors taken into consideration included both the personal characteristics and characteristics related to on-the-job performance of the employees.

2. **Stage 2: Injection of objectivity and openness:** In this phase, efforts were made to inject some objectivity in the assessments. Besides inclusion of

the traits in the rating scale, several other factors were considered by many organizations that could measure the performance efficiency and effectiveness of an employee in quantifiable terms such as targets achieved, cost savings made, suggestions introduced etc. Thus, while rating an appraisee on various personality traits continued, due weightage was also given to the accomplishments of the employee being assessed. In many systems, even the self-assessment by the employee was also introduced. In the areas where self-assessment conflicted with the assessment made by the immediate boss, the boss's boss was authorized to give the final decision overruling the decision of the employee or the immediate assessor. Feedback was given to employee and certain organizations also started linking the appraisals to the training needs of the employee.

3. **Stage 3: MBO based assessment:** This phase started the era of carrying out performance appraisals as a part and within the larger ambit of performance management. Performance management was introduced using the business

system called "management by objectives (MBO)".

Organizations started formulating their vision and mission statements and working out their business targets/goals called the objectives strictly in quantitative terms. The quantification of objectives was done in SMART way; SMART being the acronym for goals/objectives to be specific, measurable, achievable (agreed), realistic and time bound. The managers/employees of the organization were asked to project their departmental and individual objectives (in SMART way) in tandem with organizational objectives thus linking the performance targets of the employees with the organizational goals. And then their performance evaluation was done by comparing the actual objectives met by them as against the planned objectives.

But this assessment was carried out only top down. Only the superiors would carry out the appraisal. The direct reports, peers, internal customers, external customers and any other stakeholder did not have any say in the matter. Also, the processes or methods of achieving the objectives were of no concern. One could achieve the objectives even by circumventing the laid down business processes and that person was rated high if he accomplished the objectives. Result orientation alone was given the highest importance and that too as judged by the immediate superiors. So, this phase of performance management and performance appraisal had its own lacunae.

4. **Stage 4: Process and customer focus:** In order bring in more objectivity and process orientation (in addition to already established result orientation using MBO type systems) the multi-rater systems were brought into play. In addition to boss's assessment and self-assessment, assessment of an appraisee would be done also by the internal and external customers and other stakeholders. Also, the appraisers would be asked to appraise the appraisee not only on his achievements of objectives (goals/targets) but also on how well he followed the organizational, business and technical processes. This would also include assessing him on his competencies and skill sets as against the

competencies and skill sets demanded by his job. That gave rise to systems called "360 degrees", "540 degrees" and "720 degrees" performance appraisal and feedback systems. Now an appraisee could be assessed by his boss, boss's superiors, peers, direct reports, internal customers, external customers, suppliers and other appropriate stakeholders.

In addition to the multi-rater system and assessing against the goals/objectives (most of the time purely financial objectives), many organizations implemented more rounded ways of performance management approach that included more perspectives of organizational performance and growth. "Balanced Scorecard" is one such system that was suggested by Robert S Kaplan and David P Norton.

Under "Balanced Scorecard" system, organizational and therefore, individual performance is viewed from four perspectives:

- Learning and growth

- Business processes
- Customers
- Financial

It's process of implementation works as follows:

- Put the vision and strategy of the organization in the center and work out all the other details from the above-mentioned four perspectives around them.
- Under each perspective ask questions as given against each bullet below and decide objectives, measures, targets and initiatives for that specific perspective.
- *Financial perspective:* What should we do to succeed financially with reference to our stakeholders? What will be our objectives? How will we measure? What are the quantifiable targets then? What initiatives should we adopt to go about achieving them?
- *Customer perspective:* How should we relate to our customers to meet the top-level vision and in line with strategies? Then

decide about objectives, measures, targets and initiatives as we did for financial perspectives.

- *Business processes perspective:* What business processes we should be best at and improve in order to satisfy the stakeholders and customers? Subsequently decide the objectives, measures, targets and initiatives in businesses processes area.

- *Learning and growth perspective:* How will we ensure sustenance to learn, improve and grow to meet the vision? Then, work out the objectives, measures, targets and initiatives for this.

- These processes should be followed at each hierarchical level of an organization.

- The appraisal of people and departments can be done by scoring out the actual performances vis-a-vis planned against each perspective. Also, corrective actions can be initiated in time.

Later "Assessment Centers" were also introduced.

Many Appraisal Systems

Thus, many kinds of specific appraisal systems were designed and implemented by different organizations from time to time as the performance management and performance appraisal concepts and practices underwent the maturity continuum mentioned earlier. These are summarized below:

- Confidential reports by boss(es) or superior(s) on personality attributes or traits.
- Appraisal by boss(es) or superior(s) on personality attributes or traits: not strictly confidential. The traits may be given weightages and the appraisee is rated on a scale of 1 to 5 or 1 to 10.
- Appraisal by superior(s) and self: but appraiser and appraisee do not consult or discuss. Appraisal is based on ratings on personality traits as well as the accomplishments of the appraisee.
- Appraisal by superior(s) and self (appraisee) followed by a discussion between superior and appraisee to arrive at a consensus on performance rating: open appraisal (conflicting ratings are reviewed by the boss's boss and his ruling stays). It

is also referred as 180 degrees appraisal.

- Appraisal as guided by MBO (Management by Objectives: result focus) by bosses.

- Appraisal considering results and attributes/traits by superiors, self and may be, by one or two internal customers.

- Appraisal considering results, attributes and competencies/skill sets (result focus as well as process focus) by superiors, self and may be by, one or two internal customers.

- Three sixty degrees (360 degrees) performance appraisal by superiors, self, peers, direct reports, internal customers and external customers and may be suppliers and other interested stakeholders. When suppliers and other interested stakeholders are included as appraiser or raters, it is also termed as 540 degrees appraisal system.

- 720 degrees performance appraisal: Evaluation of a manager/employee is done through the 360 degrees system followed by detailed personal interviews with performance evaluators. It concentrates on what matters most to the organization. For example, the customers' or clients' views on employee's performance may be most important to the organization. Feedback is given to the employee, targets are set and necessary training is organized to help employee achieve the targets. Then the performance is evaluated again by another round of 360 degrees system based on the targets that were set during the first appraisal. The feedback and necessary guidance are given to the employee to help improve the performance.

Pitfalls in Performance Appraisals in Practice

- *Poorly trained appraisers:* In absence of lack of sufficient and correct knowledge of organization's performance appraisal process the managers responsible for evaluating their employees may commit mistakes. The process of performance appraisal can differ from organization to organization and may undergo changes from time to time. Hence the managers should be constantly kept informed and appropriate training be provided to them. The training should include the following aspects:

  - Method and guidelines for setting

34

objectives/goals.

- How to observe and measure the performance and track results.

- How to evaluate and rate the performance.

- How to maintain objectivity in assessment.

- How to structure the appraisal interviews with the employees, provide the feedback and respond to employee reactions.

- How to maintain and boost motivation and morale throughout the appraisal process.

• *Lack or absence of objectivity or increased subjectivity:* Even to date the performance appraisal suffers from rating the employees subjectively in absence of any clear-cut quantifiable criteria against which to evaluate an employee. Job descriptions/specifications, job expectations, technical and soft competencies required for the job and goals/targets to be achieved by the employee are not laid down very precisely and clearly. So, the employee gets rated on his general traits or qualities displayed in his day-to-day behavior with the boss. And that is highly subjective way of evaluation.

- *Unclear standards or lack of uniform criteria:* In absence of clarity of standards of evaluation and their uniformity across the organization, the employees may see through the haphazardness within the ratings made.

- *Central tendency:* It is one of the most commonly found pitfalls. Good majority of the appraisers or raters give average ratings to all or rate the apraisees towards the center of the rating scale. The main reason for them to do so is that if they give a very high rating or a very low rating, they may be asked by the management to provide the supporting explanations, which in turn may invite questions, criticisms or further explanations. So, they find ticking out the average rating safe. Another reason is the lack of sufficient knowledge of the employee being rated and so the appraiser does not want to err on lower or upper side of the rating scale.

- *Inconsistency in ratings:* The appraisers or raters rate the employees based on their own frame of expectations and subjectivity of judgment. There are strict raters and there are lenient raters. So, the raters whose expectations from their employees are high have a tendency to rate their employees low and the raters who get satisfied by a generally acceptable performance have a tendency to rate their employees high. Thus, the inter-rater parity may be absent in the appraisal process at the organizational level. This can pose problems in any organization. It further gets aggravated if the evaluation criteria used are subjective and not based on any quantifiable parameters.

- *Bias:* Personal bias of manager towards an employee can make him either a favorite or a non-preferred subordinate due to several reasons and that gets reflected in the ratings. Such an appraisal will not be a true picture of that employee and decisions related to rewards and promotions based on it will be seen with skepticism by other employees.

- *Halo effect:* The halo effect gets introduced in the appraisal process when an overall impression of an individual is judged on the basis of a single good trait. A high rating on one good trait leads automatically to high rating on all other traits. One good trait overshadows the other traits. Also, a very high rating may be given to protect an employee for whom there may be personal sympathy.

- *Horns effect:* The horns effect gets introduced in the appraisal process when an overall impression of an individual is judged on the basis of a single bad trait. A high rating on one bad trait leads automatically to low ratings on all other traits. One bad trait overshadows the other traits. Also, a very low rating may be given to penalize an employee for whom there may be an already negative bias.

- *Disproportionate impact of recent events on evaluation:* Raters are likely to be influenced by the more recent performance of an employee or just few isolated previous performances. They may forget or ignore many performances that need to be taken into account while assessing an employee. Thus, the performance appraisals in such cases is not the true reflection of the employee's evaluation and decisions taken based on it would be erroneous.

- *Managers' reluctance to use their scarce time and effort on the appraisal system:* A good number of managers see performance evaluation more as a ritual than the necessity. There could be several reasons for it- most important being absence of explicit buy-in of the necessity and modalities of the appraisal system by the managers, poorly designed appraisal systems involving bulky paper work and lack of time and desire to attend to it seriously. Under such situations they do not see themselves as a party to appraisal system, do not take its ownership and see it as a time-consuming ritual.

- *Employee resistance:* Many managers are reluctant to make negative or adverse ratings for fear of resistance from or confrontation with their subordinates. They lack the necessary skills to do so. In such cases the weaknesses of the employees are not brought out, correct feedback is not available and the organization suffers.

- *Lack of employee's trust in the appraisal system:* The cumulative negative impact of the pitfalls of the appraisal systems (described above) creates distrust among the employees. Skepticism seeps in naturally. Therefore, the intended aims of appraisals in terms of them being just, impartial, motivating and developmental get lost. The organization and the employees do not get the kind and quantum of advantages that a really effective appraisal system is capable of giving.

- *Partial coverage by the system:* In many organizations the top management and senior managers are kept out of the performance appraisal system's ambit. This poses a question in the minds of rest of the managers and employees. It will be a good idea if the top and senior managers lead by example by presenting themselves for appraisal.

Superior Most Systems

A combination of the following two will deliver the most optimal performance appraisal system.

- Appraisal considering results i.e. against key performance areas (KPAs), key result areas (KRAs or objectives) as well as considering the processes i.e. employee attributes and desired competencies/skill sets. Thus both, the result-focus and the process-focus become part of the system.

- Appraisal using the three sixty degrees performance appraisal and leadership system i.e. appraisal not only by the immediate boss or self evaluation but also by the peers, direct reports, internal customers and external customers.

Requirements of a Good Appraisal System

Following are the features of a good performance appraisal system:

1. It should be easily understandable by all the concerned. It should not be complex or time consuming.
2. It should be organization specific. Each organization aims at its own vision, mission, objectives and short term and log term goals. Appraisal system should complement those specific organizational efforts.
3. It must have an explicit acceptance and support from all the concerned.

4. The system should have been validated. The employee ratings that are churned out through an appraisal should truly and fully reflect the level of competency, process orientation and result orientation of an employee rated by the system. System should provide for the objective assessment.

5. The system should be open and participative sans any ulterior motives.

6. System should have inbuilt motivational pull and push in order for the employees and their supervising managers to look at it with interest and enthusiasm.

Rating Scales

Following rating scale is often used to rate the employees against their various traits, competencies/skill-sets requirements and the quantifiable goals to be achieved by the employees:

- Unsatisfactory (well below the requirements of the position)
- Needs improvement (below requirements of the position)

- Meets job requirements (fully meets requirements of the position)
- Exceeds job requirements (above requirements of the position)
- Outstanding (well above requirements of the position)

Organization may adopt any other scale as appropriate.

Post Appraisal Actions

Based on the performance appraisals, which are normally done annually in most of the organizations, following actions are taken by the managements of the organizations. HR departments often play as coordinators and links in the entire appraisal process and the post appraisal actions.

1. *Rewards and awards:* Various types of motivational packages are designed and used by different organizations. Based on the appraisal of an employee, he is given non-monetary and monetary awards and rewards. The management decides the financial budgets for this purpose and the awards and rewards are controlled within such budgets.

This kind of constraint often compels the appraising managers to compromise on their ratings of the even deserving employees and this often creates dissatisfaction among them. At times the dissatisfied bright employee may even decide to quit the organization thus incurring a great loss of human capital to the organization.

Management often gives certain guidelines on how many persons can be accommodated in the budgets and in what proportions. An example of the representative guidelines often issued by many organizations is given below (percentages specified in the example may vary):

- 1% of employees in the top most category of awards/rewards in terms of performance
- 14% of employees in the next superior category of awards/rewards in terms of performance
- 70% of employees in the average category of awards/rewards in terms of performance
- 14% of employees in the below average category of awards/rewards in terms of performance

- 1% of employees in the lowest category of awards/rewards in terms of performance

Awards and rewards may include promotions, up-gradation of job titles, superior office space/furniture, superior housing, salary raises, enhanced perquisites, stock options, bonuses, profit sharing, company paid holidays and excursions etc.

2. *Transfers, job rotations/job enrichment, foreign assignments and postings:* Based on the assessment of the present and the potential performances of the employees, certain employees may be given new responsibilities through job transfers, job rotations/job enrichment, deputations to foreign assignments and postings etc.

3. *Training and development:* Performance appraisal is used to carry out the training needs analysis (also known as development needs analysis). Based on the analysis, employees are trained and developed appropriately as per the needs of the organization. This is a very important outcome of the appraisal process and proves beneficial to the organization as

well as to the employees. Apart from the conventional on-the-job and classroom training methods other methods that are employed for development of employees are mentoring, counseling and coaching.

4. *Disciplining:* At times performance appraisal points at the needs of disciplining the employees based on which the identified undisciplined persons are counseled and disciplined.

5. *Separations:* In some situations when a particular employee is repetitively rated an unsatisfactory performer in successive performance appraisals, organization may decide to show him the door.

Designing a Performance Appraisal Form

Performance appraisal form provides the basis for performance review, giving feedback to employee about his performance and post performance review plans for him. Therefore, performance appraisal form should be designed carefully and filled with utmost care and objectivity.

Normally the immediate manager of the employee and the employee himself fill the performance appraisal form. However, in multi-rater systems direct reports, peers, internal customers, external customers, vendors/suppliers and other related stakeholders also fill it. At the end, all the forms filled by all these different evaluators are collated and a consolidated picture of the employee's assessment is arrived at.

Each organization will need to design its own performance appraisal form as per its specific requirements and objectives. Simply copying a form from a reference book or from other organizations and using it is not appropriate and may create more problems than advantages. Therefore, it will not be appropriate to suggest any specific format here. So, what we are giving below are only the guidelines to design an effective form.

We are suggesting here a form that contains five parts:

Part 1 of the form:

This part should include the identification details of the assessee/appraisee. Details like name, employee ID, department, position title, grade and performance review period can be included in this part.

Part 2 of the form:

This part should be designed to document the achievements of the employee in quantitative and non-quantitative or descriptive/narrative terms against the goals/targets set for the employee. Both, the expected goals and goals achieved by the employee should be registered. Then against each of these goals, columns should be provided to rate the employee by the rater on a scale of 1 to 5, 1 denoting unsatisfactory performance and 5 meaning the outstanding performance with 2, 3 and 4 categorized as below average, average and above average performances.

Essentially this part of the form has the result focus.

Part 3 of the form:

This part of the form lists down the technical and soft competencies required for the performing the job. The rater(s) rate how good the employee is at these competencies and how well the employee uses these competencies (the process aspects).

Several descriptive statements that define each competency/process can be placed in the form under each competency/process so as to facilitate the rater to rate the employee against each competency/process. For example, to rate the appraisee for his competency on "Quality" following statements can be specified in the appraisal form under the competency/process called "Quality":

- Tries to achieve right the first time avoiding any rework/rejection.
- Committed to excellence in work.
- Adopts new processes to achieve better quality.
- Champion of the six-sigma system introduced in the organization.
- Follows the laid down technical and business processes.

Thus, essentially this part presents the competencies/skill sets and process focus.

Depending on the specific competency/process needs of the organization different competencies/skill sets are included for different hierarchical levels and different functions of the organization. Some examples of competencies included are: job knowledge, initiative and self starting capability, planning and organizing, analytical skills and problem solving, quality consciousness, leading and motivating, interpersonal skills, communication, delegation, team building and team work, time management, efficiency, cost effectiveness, creativity and innovation, use of technology and the required specific technical/functional competencies.

As mentioned in earlier paragraph, the employee is rated on a scale of 1 to 5, 1 denoting unsatisfactory performance and 5 meaning the outstanding performance with 2, 3 and 4 categorized as below average, average and above average performances.

Part 4 of the form:

This part provides for additional descriptive comments the raters may like to make regarding the appraisee. It can further be divided into two parts. In the first part the raters can be asked to documents the existing strengths of the employee giving examples of the actual events that demonstrate these strengths. In the second part they can be asked to list out the areas where they think there is a need and scope of further improvements in the employee and what they suggest could be done to bring about the improvements.

Part 5 of the form: This part has the provision for documenting the overall rating of the employee. Overall rating for the assessee is determined based on the ratings given by the assessor against each competency and the assessment of the employee for his achievements/goal accomplishments.

The determination of the overall rating is not a pure arithmetic since many areas of the appraisal remain subjective due to non-availability of numerical standards of performance in such areas. So, the subjective judgment of the assessor plays some part in deciding the overall rating.

Overall rating can be expressed in terms of following gradations on the scale ranging from 1 to 5:

- 1- Unsatisfactory (well below the requirements of the position)
- 2- Needs improvement (below requirements of the

position)

- 3- Meets job requirements (fully meets requirements of the position)
- 4- Exceeds job requirements (above requirements of the position)
- 5- Outstanding (well above requirements of the position)

Organizations may use any other scale as appropriate.

Performance Review Meeting

The performance review meeting is held between the appraisee (the employee) and the appraiser (the manager) in a congenial, supporting and open environment using two-way communication. The purpose of performance review meeting is to provide feedback on the outcome of the appraisal process to the concerned employee and reach mutually agreed conclusions for further improvement regarding his performance and development. Also, the modalities of achieving this are discussed and decided.

Managers should use the performance review meetings to motivate their employees to perform better in future.

Review meetings ideally should include the following:

- Review of progress on tasks and activities in relation to the employee's performance plan.
- The initiatives taken by the employee himself and those planned by the management for the employee.
- Identification of variances in terms of delays, requisite quality and shortfall in support/guidance/help planned for the employee.
- Analyzing the causes of the delay, the problems faced and the solutions adopted.
- Preparation of action steps for solving identified problems and contingency plans for anticipated problems.

The manner of giving the feedback of the performance to the employee is very important. The conversation should have an optimistic and motivating tone. Therefore, some important points that should be observed by the managers in the active performance appraisal conversation are:

- Make it a dialogue and not just a one-way communication. An effective performance appraisal review requires an interactive discussion with an open agenda. Give employee a fair chance to put forward his ideas.

- Ensure that the discussion involves a full, free and frank exchange of views about what has been achieved, what needs to be done to achieve more.

- Be a good listener. Listen to the employee's ideas and problems. Understand his body language.

- Address what's important to the employee for furthering his growth and what is of value to the organization.

- Start the review meeting with affirming the employee's strengths. Do not hesitate in acknowledging how much you value his contributions.

- Don't be confrontational. Also do not to criticize the employee in general terms. Focus on evaluating his job performance in specific terms. Otherwise the session may turn into a grievance session missing the opportunity to raise employee's motivation and morale level.

- Do make constructive criticisms with guidance on ways to improve.

- Reach an agreement. Jointly come to an understanding about what has to be done by both parties to improve performance, knowledge and skills and overcome any work problems raised during the discussion.

- If an employee misses an expected rating and promotion/raise, do not make false promises to him that you would surely take care of his interests in future.

Frequency of Appraisals

The most conventional practice in majority of the organization is to carry out the performance appraisal of their employees annually. However, some experts feel that the appraisals if administered more frequently (say, every six months or even every month, though the formal documentation can be done twice a year to minimize time consuming paperwork) may have positive outcomes for employees as well as the organization. This way employees do not feel and face the year-end shocks and surprises thrown at them by the usual once a year type appraisal ritual. More frequent reviews are more proactive in nature and organizations can take preemptive performance improvement measures well in time.

Some other experts propose annual appraisals for employees deployed on routine type of jobs and more frequent appraisals for the people on non-routine, creative and project type of jobs.

Performance Appraisal: Dynamic Process

In any forward-looking organization, its current performance appraisal system that looks quite effective today may not look so good in the coming years. Dynamism in several business factors compels a periodic review of an appraisal system. Ever changing customer requirements, business competitiveness, technologies, knowledge and competency levels of the people etc will have a significant impact on the modalities of a performance appraisal system. This area should be continually examined and studied in order to bring about changes in the performance appraisal system to keep it relevant and useful all the time. Only then the appraisal system will continue to be beneficial for any organization.

Anti Views on Performance Appraisal

While almost every organization implements performance

appraisal system in some form or other as a necessary compulsion in absence of any other better system for the purpose, employees and managers have never accepted the appraisal systems wholeheartedly. They do not perceive the appraisal systems as any great systems capable of bringing in genuine objectivity or acting as an effective motivational force.

So, there exist many documented anti views on the appraisal systems. The views given below are mainly based on opinions of Peter Scholtes and Edward Deming:

- Data and research are not available to show that performance appraisal does any good. There is no evidence to indicate that a company that uses performance appraisal does any better than it would if it did not use performance appraisal.
- It is reported that, when quality guru Edwards Deming was asked what to do about performance appraisals, he replied, "Whatever Peter Scholtes says."
- Performance appraisal and a number of other management interventions are based on a fairly cynical premise about people by those who manage.

The view that gets reflected is: we would be okay if it weren't for the inadequacies of our individual employees.

- As per Deming, systems are the cause of problems and the cause of solutions. If you want to improve what you are doing, you have to improve your systems. You should not think organizations as hierarchies (the conventional view). As per Scholtes, if you want to improve, what you do is to improve the system; you don't pester the people to work harder or work smarter. You don't threaten them with punishment or promise them rewards, that's looking in the wrong place.

- Performance appraisal tends to undermine the system (process) by encouraging individuals to organize their performance often at the expense of the system.

- Performance appraisal can undermine teams because many times, individuals want to look good at the expense of the team.

- At times, performance appraisal makes an employee totally boss oriented irrespective of the system (process) or team.

- Performance appraisal is supposed to provide

channels of communication and feedback to the employees but in real practice that hardly happens.

- So, what to do? If an organization has a performance appraisal system, should it just throw it out the window and start working on the transition to systems thinking? "That's a pretty good start," says Scholtes. "Most people hate performance appraisal, but they assume that's because they are not doing it the right way. There is no right way to do it, it's inherently the wrong thing to do."

www.ingramcontent.com/pod-product-compliance
Lightning Source LLC
Chambersburg PA
CBHW071637170526
45166CB00003B/1351